The BAKER'S WIFE
a musical

Music
and
Lyrics by
Stephen Schwartz

T0079075

Artwork Courtesy of Richard Green & Greg MacKellan

ISBN: 978-1-4234-1103-1

WILLIAMSON MUSIC®
A RODGERS AND HAMMERSTEIN COMPANY
www.williamsonmusic.com

EXCLUSIVELY DISTRIBUTED BY

HAL•LEONARD®
CORPORATION
7777 W. BLUEMOUND RD. P.O. BOX 13819 MILWAUKEE, WI 53213

In Australia Contact:
Hal Leonard Australia Pty. Ltd.
4 Lentara Court
Cheltenham, Victoria, 3192 Australia
Email: ausadmin@halleonard.com

The offering of this publication for sale is not to be construed as authorization for the performance of any material contained herein.
Applications for the right to perform *The Baker's Wife*, in whole or in part, should be addressed to:

MUSIC THEATRE INTERNATIONAL
421 W. 54th St.
New York, New York 10019
Tel 212/541-4MTI • Fax 212/5X7-4MTI
Website: www.mtishows.com

Williamson Music is a registered trademark of the Family Trust u/w Richard Rodgers and the Estate of Oscar Hammerstein II.

Visit Hal Leonard Online at
www.halleonard.com

CONTENTS

STEPHEN SCHWARTZ

Stephen Schwartz has contributed music and/or lyrics to *Wicked, Godspell, Pippin, The Magic Show, The Baker's Wife, Working* (which he also adapted and directed), *Personals, Rags,* and *Children of Eden.* He collaborated with Leonard Bernstein on the English texts for Bernstein's *Mass* and wrote the title song for the play and movie *Butterflies Are Free.* For films, he wrote the songs for the DreamWorks animated feature *Prince of Egypt* and collaborated with Alan Menken on the scores for the Disney animated features *Pocahontas* and *The Hunchback of Notre Dame.* For children, he has written a one-act musical, *Captain Louie,* and a picture book, *The Perfect Peach.* Mr. Schwartz has released two CDs of original songs entitled *Reluctant Pilgrim* and *Uncharted Territory.* Among the awards he has received are three Academy Awards, four Grammy Awards, four Drama Desk Awards, and a Golden Globe.

CHANSON

Music and Lyrics by
STEPHEN SCHWARTZ

Gently

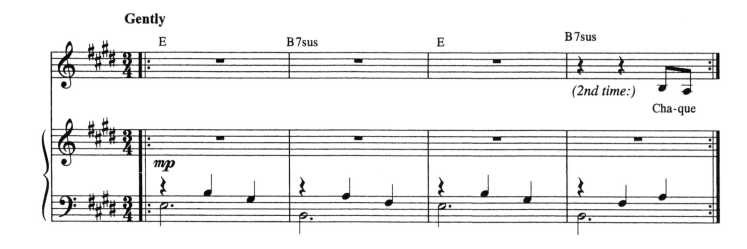

(2nd time:)

Cha-que

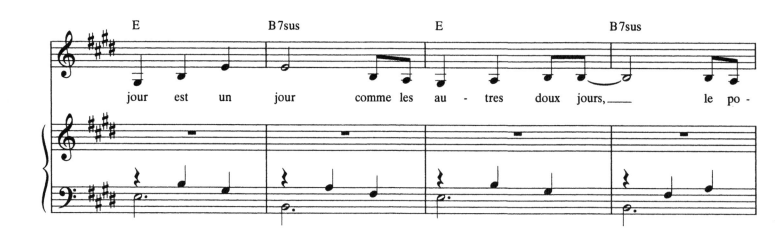

jour est un jour comme les au - tres doux jours,____ le po-

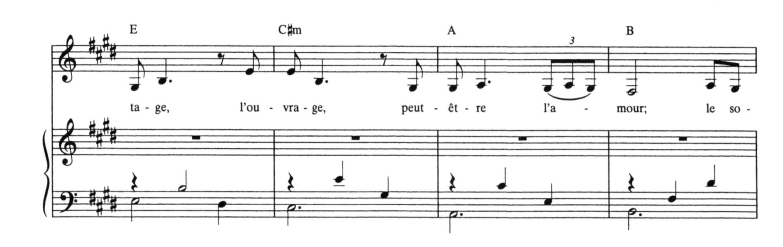

ta - ge, l'ou - vra - ge, peut - êt - re l'a - mour; le so-

leil, il voy - a - ge, le monde fait un tour, ain - si c'est tou-

jours le mê - me. _____ 1. Ev - 'ry

day as you do what you do ev - 'ry day, ___ you see the same
wind chang - es course, and the moon chang - es phase, ___ and the world spins a -

fac - es who fill the ca - fé; and if some of those
round with the greens and the ___ grays, and you nev - er take

6

now your whole life is new.

La la la la la la

la la la la. La la la la la la

GIFTS OF LOVE
(Pop Version)

Music and Lyrics by
STEPHEN SCHWARTZ

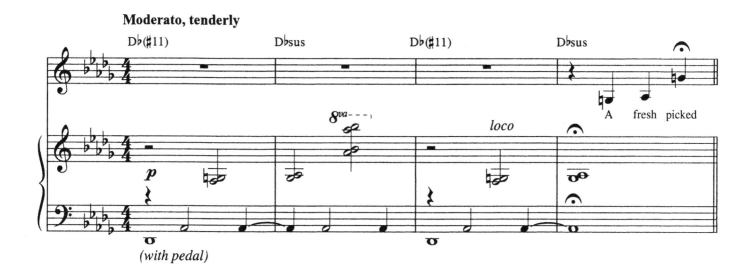

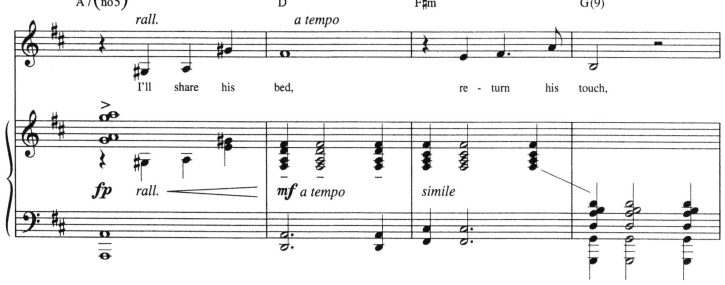

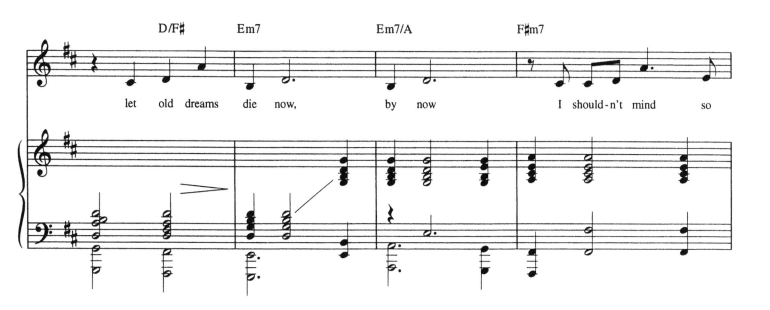

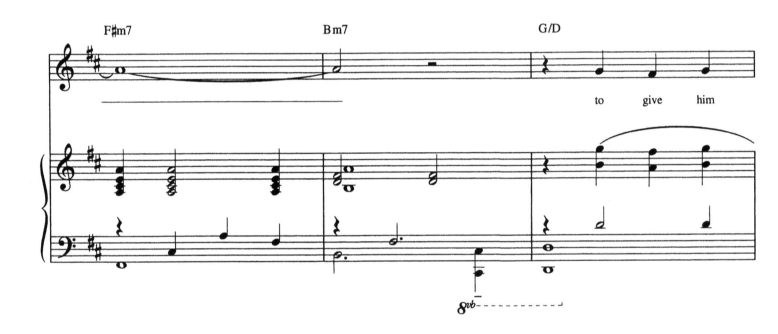

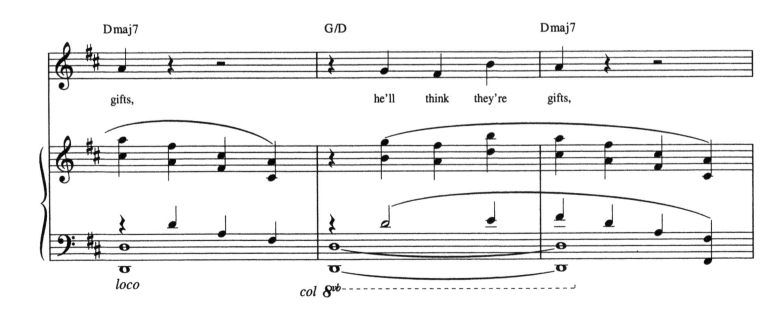

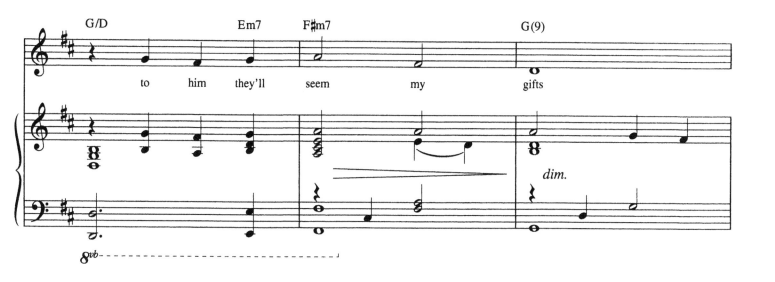

to him they'll seem my gifts

of love.

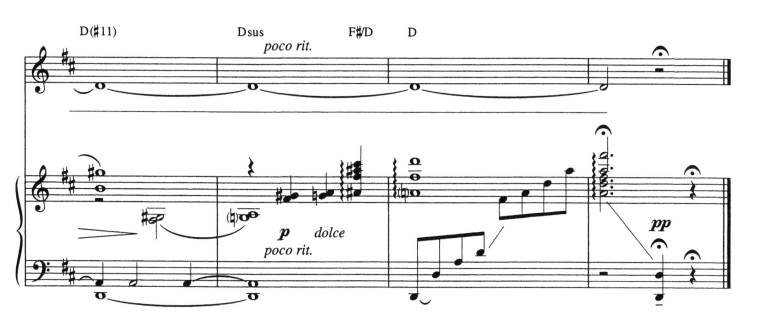

PROUD LADY

Music and Lyrics by
STEPHEN SCHWARTZ

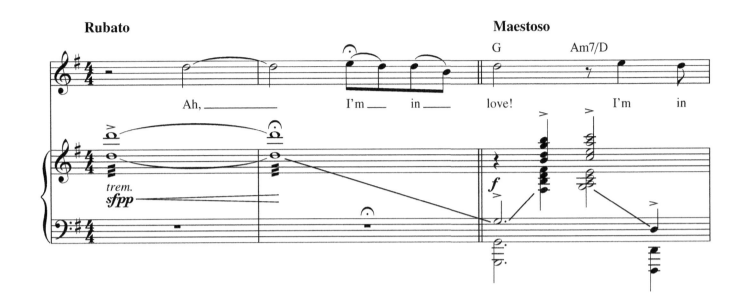

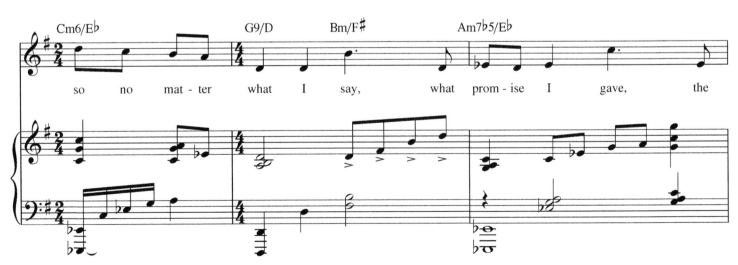

* See page 27 for alternate ending

Alternate ending
Maestoso

life! _____

love! I'm in love a-gain! I'm in ___ love, I'm in love, and

is -n't it a crime? Is -n't it a cry - ing shame that the

love of my life should have to be an - oth - er man's wife? But I've

fi - n'ly found the one true love of my life

for the twen-ty third time!

MEADOWLARK

Music and Lyrics by
STEPHEN SCHWARTZ

voice could match the an - gels' in its glor - y, but she was

blind, the lark was blind. An

old king came and took her to his pal - ace where the

walls were bur - nished bronze and gol - den braid. And he

fed her fruit and nuts ___ from an iv - 'ry cha - lice ___ and he

prayed: ___ "Sing ___ for

accelerando poco a poco

1.me ___ my mea-dow - lark, ___
2.me ___ my mea-dow - lark, ___

sing for me ___ of the sil - ver
fly with me ___ on the sil - ver

2nd time
To Coda ⊕

sing _____ for _____ me."
fly _____ with _____ me."

Then one day as the lark ___

___ sang by the wa - ter, _____ the

God of the sun heard her in his flight _____

and her sing-ing moved him so he came and

brought her ___ the gift ___ of sight. _____

___

He gave __ her sight ___ and she

o-pened her eyes __ to the shim-mer _____ and the splen - dor _____

of this beau - ti - ful ___ young God, so proud and

strong. ___ And he called to the lark in a

voice both rough ___ and ten - der. ___ "Come a -

D. S. 𝄋 *al Coda* ⊕

long. ___ Fly with

8va bassa

king came down that ____ day, ____

subito **p**

mea - dow - lark ____ had died.

Ev -'ry time I heard ____ that part I ____ cried. ____

crescendo ____

sf p

Col 8va bassa _ _ _ _ _ _ _ _ |

loco

(crescendo) ____

And

8va bassa

38

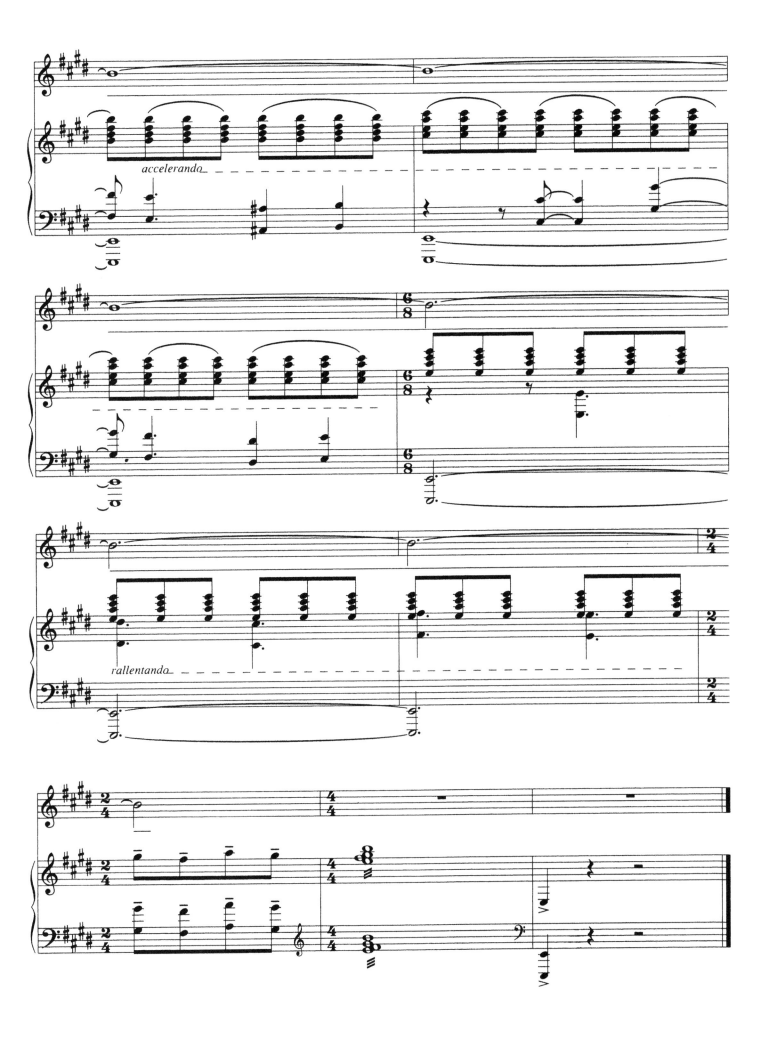

IF I HAVE TO LIVE ALONE

Music and Lyrics by
STEPHEN SCHWARTZ

Andante

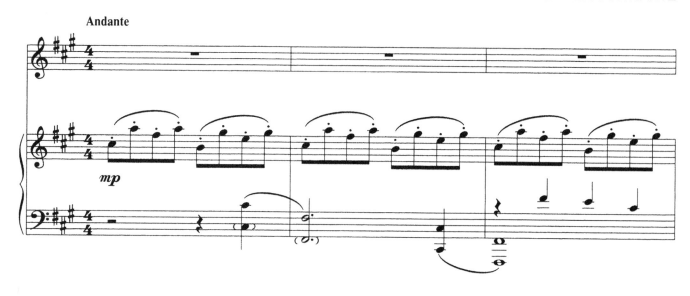

The house seems small -er   since she's been gone.   The lights stay dim   and the

shut -ters   drawn.   But the clock keeps run -ning   and time   runs   on,   and there's

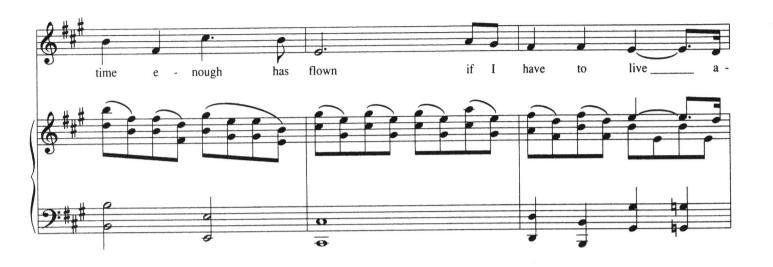

time e - nough has flown if I have to live _____ a -

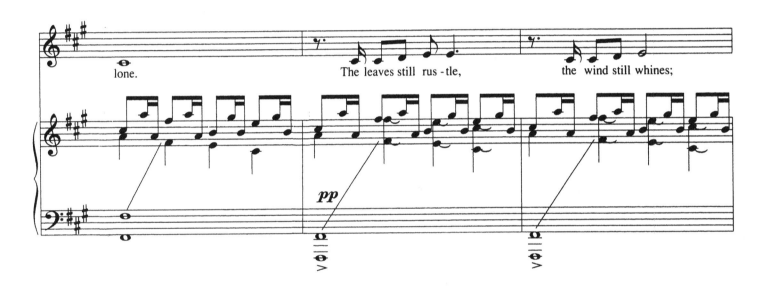

lone. The leaves still rus - tle, the wind still whines;

pp

the sun shines cold -er but still it shines. I do my liv - ing be -

tween the lines __ like the si - lent times I've known when I

had to live _____ a - lone. _____

Be -fore I knew her I had my ways __ to fill the hours, __

to kill the days. Have a meal at the ca - fe ev - 'ry night at ten; take a

walk, take a nap, per - haps a card game now and then.

I've lived a - lone __ be - fore and I can do it a - gain.

A tempo

I still hear laughter, I still see stars, and if it's true ___ that a

smile comes hard, well, that's the reas-on that God made scars, to pro-

tect us once they've grown. Let them hard-en now like

stone, let them hard - en now like stone if I

have to ___ live ___ a - lone. ___

WHERE IS THE WARMTH

Music and Lyrics by
STEPHEN SCHWARTZ

Look at him, ___ that's a tor - so that's rare. When I look at him ___ how I burn to be touch-ing him; ___ the fire ___ is there. ___ But where is the warmth?

Look at us, ___ don't you think we fit beau-ti-f'ly to - geth-er?

Look at us, ___ can't you see how we shine? When you

look at us, ___ do you no-tice I'm shiv-er-ing? The weath-er is

fine. ___ But where is the

look at me, you would think this the crue-lest of Dec - em -bers.

a tempo

Look at me, ___ you would think we'd had snow. Then he

rit

looks at me ___ and for a mo - ment I melt a -gain; ___ the em - bers do ___

8va

loco

___ glow. _____ But oh, where is the

a tempo

f

56